LADY | GAGA  *The Fame*

ISBN 978-1-4234-8109-6

HAL•LEONARD®
CORPORATION
7777 W. BLUEMOUND RD. P.O. BOX 13819 MILWAUKEE, WI 53213

Visit Hal Leonard Online at
www.halleonard.com

4 **Just Dance**

12 **LoveGame**

19 **Paparazzi**

24 **Poker Face**

30 **Eh, Eh (Nothing Else I Can Say)**

35 **Beautiful, Dirty, Rich**

39 **The Fame**

45 **Money Honey**

50 **Starstruck**

58 **Boys Boys Boys**

63 **Paper Gangsta**

70 **Brown Eyes**

75 **I Like It Rough**

80 **Summerboy**

JUST DANCE

Words and Music by STEFANI GERMANOTTA,
RedOne and ALIAUNE THIAM

dance, __ spin that rec - ord, babe. Da da do do. ____ Just

dance. _ (Spoken:) Amazing music... Wooh!

Let's go! Half psy-chot-ic, sick hyp-not - ic, got my blue-print, it's sym - phon -

ic. Half psy-chot-ic, sick hyp-not - ic, got my blue-print e - lec-tron - ic. Half psy-chot-ic, sick hyp-not -

LOVEGAME

Words and Music by STEFANI GERMANOTTA
and RedOne

Moderate Dance groove

Let's have some fun, this beat is sick. I wan-na take a ride on your dis - co stick. Let's

have some fun, this beat is sick. I wan - na take a ride on your dis - co stick.

Huh,

huh. ___

PAPARAZZI

Words and Music by STEFANI GERMANOTTA
and ROB FUSARI

POKER FACE

Words and Music by STEFANI GERMANOTTA
and RedOne

Dance Pop

EH, EH
(Nothing Else I Can Say)

Words and Music by STEFANI GERMANOTTA
and MARTIN KIERSZENBAUM

BEAUTIFUL, DIRTY, RICH

Words and Music by STEFANI GERMANOTTA
and ROB FUSARI

THE FAME

Words and Music by STEFANI GERMANOTTA
and MARTIN KIERSZENBAUM

MONEY HONEY

Words and Music by STEFANI GERMANOTTA,
RedOne and BILAL HAJJI

Moderate Techno groove

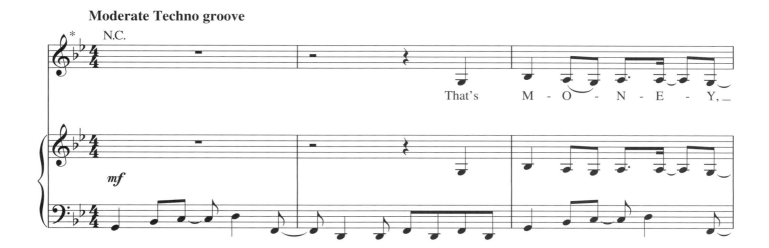

That's M-O-N-E-Y,

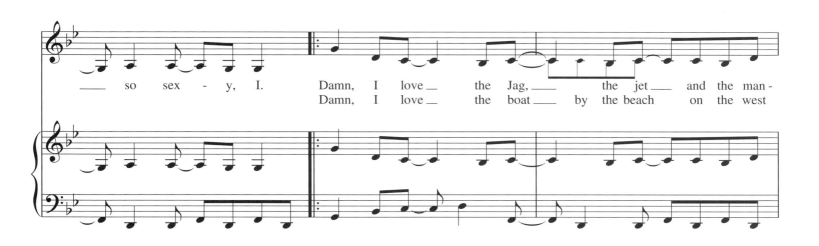

so sex-y, I.
Damn, I love the Jag, the jet and the man-
Damn, I love the boat by the beach on the west

sion, oh yeah. And I en-joy the gifts
coast, oh yeah. And I en-joy some fine

* Recorded a half step higher.

When you touch me it's so de - li - cious, _____ that's mon - ey hon - ey.

hon - ey. Ba - by, when you tear me to piec - es, that's mon - ey

hon - ey. When you give me k - hon - ey. That's M - O

N - E - Y, _____ so sex - y, I.

STARSTRUCK

Words and Music by STEFANI GERMANOTTA,
TRAMAR DILLARD, MARTIN KIERSZENBAUM
and NICK DRESTI

Recorded a half step lower.

styl- in' out to the beat that you're freak - in'. Fan - ta - size I'm the track that you're tweak - in';

blow my heart up. Put your hands on my waist, pull the fad - er.

Run it back with o - rig - i - nal fla - vor. Cue me up; I'm the 12 on your ta - ble.

Am

Fmaj7

I'm so star - struck! Star - struck, ba - by, 'cause you blow my heart up. I'm so

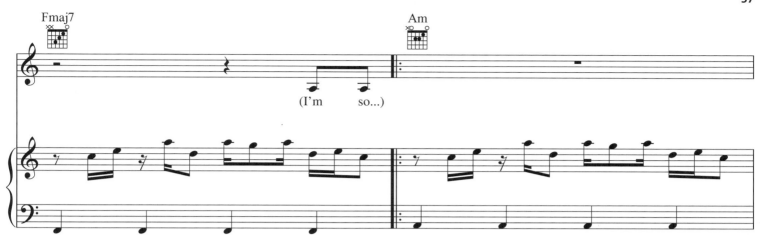

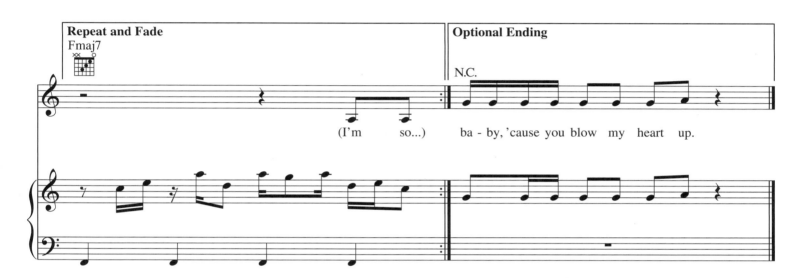

Additional Lyrics

Rap: Hey, lil momma, like really, really, is that him?
I done seen you before. What you got on them big rims?
Enter that cash flow, I'm like, baby, you don't trip.
So shawy, say hand over your signature right here.

Like on just the dotted line, and I'm supposed to sign.
How's she at it? A fanatic, and I think it's goin' down.
She so starstruck, the gal all stuck.
I should have had an overdose, too many Starbucks.

Ain't never seen a balla, paper that stack taller.
Notice who let the top back on the Chevy Impala.
Hummers and all that fully loaded with two spoilers.
What did you call that when you showed up with two dollars?

But that's another chapter, son of a bachelor.
All one me, just spotted baby actor.
Complete swagga, there go the dagger.
Got what she wants, shawty happily ever after.

BOYS BOYS BOYS

Words and Music by STEFANI GERMANOTTA
and RedOne

Dance tempo

Hey there, sug - ar ba - by, saw you twice at the pop __ show.
Ba - by is a bad boy with some ret - ro __ sneak - ers.

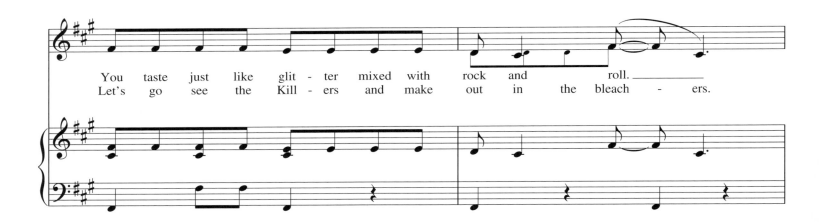

You taste just like glit - ter mixed with rock and roll. _____
Let's go see the Kill - ers and make out in the bleach - ers.

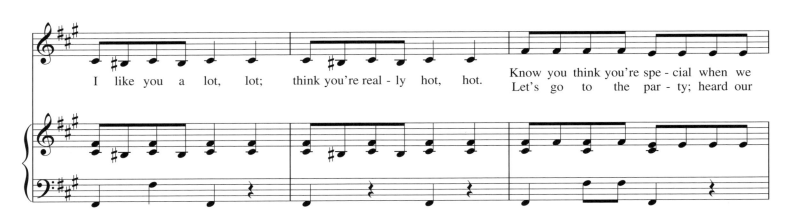

I like you a lot, lot; think you're real - ly hot, hot.
Let's go to the par - ty; heard our

Know you think you're spe - cial when we

PAPER GANGSTA

Words and Music by STEFANI GERMANOTTA
and RedOne

Recorded a half step lower.

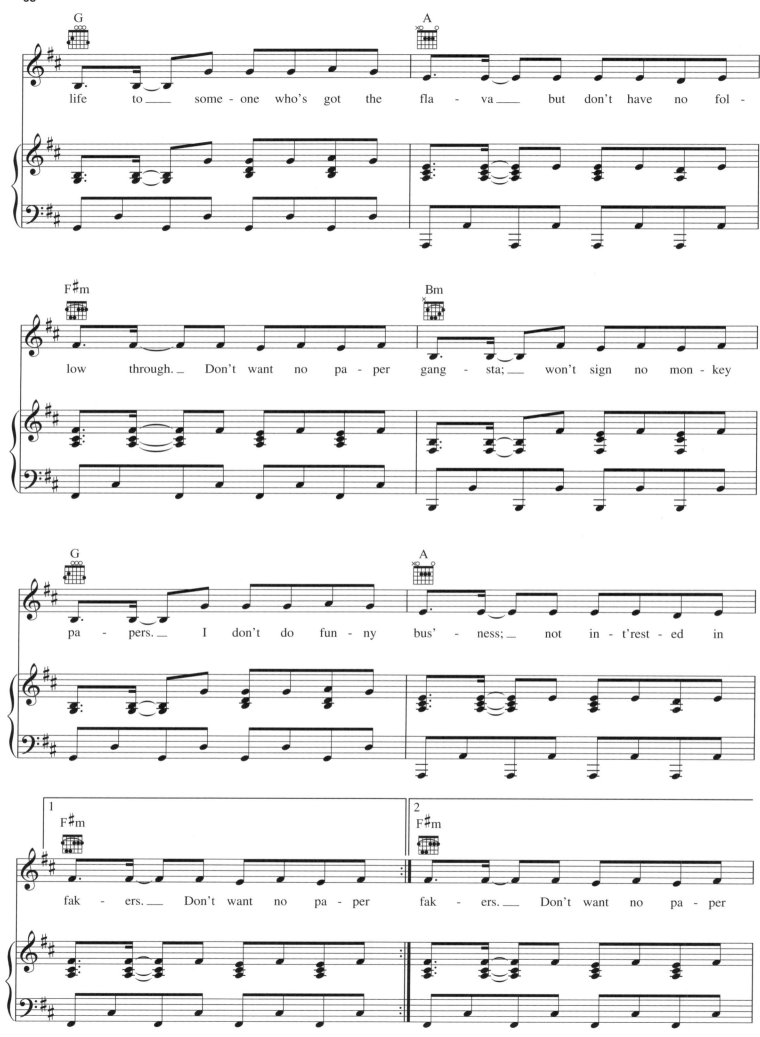

BROWN EYES

Words and Music by STEFANI GERMANOTTA
and ROB FUSARI

I LIKE IT ROUGH

Words and Music by STEFANI GERMANOTTA
and MARTIN KIERSZENBAUM

Can't sleep with the man who dims __ my shine. __
Prom girl wipes her tears with sil - ver lines, __ and she

can't get e - nough. __ I'm in the bed - room
I'm in the bed - room with tis - sues and when __ I know you're

out - side bang - ing and I won't let you in. 'Cause it's a hard __ life with

love in the world. __ And I'm a hard __ girl; lov - ing me is like
lov - ing me is like

SUMMERBOY

Words and Music by STEFANI GERMANOTTA,
BRIAN KIERULF and JOSHUA SCHWARTZ